The Cattleman's Suite

The Cattleman's Suite

A Comedy in Two Acts

Scot Lahaie

Writers Club Press
San Jose New York Lincoln Shanghai

The Cattleman's Suite
A Comedy in Two Acts

Writers Club Press
an imprint of iUniverse, Inc.

For information address:
iUniverse, Inc.
5220 S. 16th St., Suite 200
Lincoln, NE 68512
www.iuniverse.com

Any resemblance to actual people and events is purely coincidental.
This is a work of fiction.

Original copyright 1995 as an unpublished manuscript.

ISBN: 0-595-24285-5

Printed in the United States of America

Contents

Characters

DOUGLAS B. DRITHERS, a Texas Oilman

JULIE DRITHERS, his only daughter

BOBBY GRANGER, Julie's true love

BILLOWS B. SNOOKER, Drithers' best friend

SALLY SNOOKER, his wife

MATT SNOOKER, their son

MR. BRIARBUSH, the hotel manager

MR. McGRUFF, the hotel detective

JASPER, an industrial spy

FRANK, his assistant

MARY, a maid

HANNIBAL, a bellboy

Synopsis of Scenes

ACT I, Scene 1 – Mid morning on a Tuesday in May.

ACT I, Scene 2 – Several hours later, after lunch

ACT II, Scene 1 – The next evening, about 6:30 p.m.

The Setting: A hotel suite in Dallas, Texas.

The Time: The year is 1948. The month is May.

Act One

SCENE 1

The Cattleman's Suite

A hotel suite on the thirteenth floor of a Dallas four-star hotel. As the CURTAIN RISES, MARY, a maid, ENTERS from the bedroom down-stage right with an arm full of bedclothes. She has changed the beds for the incoming guests. She drops the old sheets in the laundry sack on her service cart. As she does, MR. BRIARBUSH, the hotel manager, ENTERS through the hallway door upstage center.

BRIARBUSH

There you are! Aren't you finished yet?

MARY

Yes, Mr. Briarbush, sir. Bathrooms mopped and washed, with the chrome polished up real nice. Beds aired out with new sheets, carpets vacuumed, tile floors mopped, furniture dusted and polished, the drapes were sent out for cleaning and were hung fresh this morning. Was there anything else, sir?

BRIARBUSH

No, I think that was the whole list. What about the bar and the refreshments?

MARY

It's not my area. I just do the dirty stuff.

BRIARBUSH

Right! Sorry.

MARY

Already forgotten.

BRIARBUSH

Where is that house detective hiding? McGruff!

(He pulls a seaman's whistle from his pocket and blows a three-tone whistle. A moment later McGRUFF ENTERS upstage center.)

McGRUFF

You called, Mr. Briarbush, sir?

BRIARBUSH

Yes, I did. Have you done the room security check as I asked you to?

McGRUFF

Not yet, sir. I'll get right on it! So far I've checked the register for the whole floor and all new employees are being given a background check. All that's left is to check this room.

BRIARBUSH

Well? What are you waiting for?

McGRUFF

Tell me, sir, Mr. Briarbush, sir, why all the fuss anyway? Who is so important that you have to go and clean the drapes for? Is the President coming for a visit?

BRIARBUSH

No, the President is not coming for a visit. Since you've asked, we are expecting a far more important guest. None other than Mr. Douglas B. Drithers of Drithers Oil Incorporated is arriving this morning for a three-day visit. He is the richest and most successful oilman of this great state. He is also a big tipper.

MARY

Oh! I like the sound of this.

McGRUFF

And what is the purpose of his visit? Business or pleasure?

BRIARBUSH

We have been graced with the opportunity of hosting the engagement party for his only daughter, Julie. It is not yet public knowledge, but she is to be wed to Matthew R. Snooker, son of Billows B. Snooker, owner of Snooker Industrials Incorporated, the industry's major manufacturer of drilling and piping equipment. And it will happen here in this very suite, in the Dallas Grand Hotel! Think of it!

MARY

But why this old suite of all places? There are much nicer rooms in the new wing. This one's been locked up tight for years. The dust was an inch thick on the end tables.

BRIARBUSH

My dear, I haven't all day to answer questions. But to satisfy your curiosity, twenty-eight years ago, in 1920, Mr. Drithers, Senior, held an engagement party for his son Douglas in this very suite. Mr. Drithers, being a man of nostalgia, desires to have his daughter's engagement party in the same room. More I cannot tell you. But I assure you, my pretty, whatever Mr. Douglas "Big Spender" Drithers wants, he will get.

McGRUFF

I still don't understand. Why all the fuss? We host at least six weddings a year and even more engagement parties. Why all the security?

BRIARBUSH

Mr. McGruff! It is rumored that Mr. Drithers is looking to buy into the hotel business. That is to say, he is looking to buy a hotel—a Texas hotel. It is conceivable that he could be interested in this hotel. A hotel that may go bankrupt this year, if it isn't merged with or bought by a larger company with greater resources to invest in repairs and remodeling. A closing of this hotel would do more than just impact the financial health of this community; it would mean the loss of our jobs, if I make myself clear. It is also conceivable that our competition would do just about anything to see that Mr. Drithers does not buy this hotel. I fully expect our competition to try to sabotage Mr. Drithers' stay at our fine establishment. Do you understand me now?

McGRUFF

Yes sir! We are at war and there is a potential spy on our flagship.

BRIARBUSH

Now what are you waiting for Mr. McGruff? Get to work! Mr. Drithers is due here any minute.

McGRUFF

Yes sir!

(He scrambles to the bedroom.)

BRIARBUSH

And you! Get this cart out of here! And polish the door handles on your way out!

MARY

Yes sir! Right away, sir! Thank you, sir!

(As MARY EXITS, HANNIBAL, the Bellboy, ENTERS with the refreshment on a large tray.)

HANNIBAL

Good morning, Mr. Briarbutt, sir.

BRIARBUSH

…Briarbush…bush…bush! Who the hell are you?

HANNIBAL

I'm new here, sir. You hired me last week. Don't you remember?

BRIARBUSH

Your name?

HANNIBAL

Hannibal, sir.

BRIARBUSH

Right. Of course I remember! And what do you want?

HANNIBAL

I'm here to stock the bar, sir.

BRIARBUSH

Good. Get on with it then.

HANNIBAL

…and to deliver a message from the desk.

(He reads from a small scrap of paper.)

"Mr. Drithers has just arrived. At reception. Come immediately."

BRIARBUSH

Why didn't you say so sooner?! You idiot! McGruff!!

McGRUFF

(Off.) Sir?!

(ENTERING from the bedroom.)

BRIARBUSH

Finish up here, will you. I've got to go find Drithers before the idiots at the reception spoil the whole deal.

(He EXITS.)

McGRUFF

Right, sir!

HANNIBAL.

(Stocking the bar.) Isn't he a grouch today?!

McGRUFF

He may be, but he is the boss. And it would do you well to try and not anger him. And as far as I'm concerned, I'd appreciate it if you would keep out of my way. I've got work to do and I don't need the "hired help" getting in my way.

(He EXITS to the other bedroom.)

HANNIBAL

Nice guy. What have I let myself in for? Well, let's give it a week and see how it goes. If it doesn't get better, we'll just hit the road again.

(He continues with the bar. The main door opens and BOBBY ENTERS.)

BOBBY

Hi!

HANNIBAL

Hi.

BOBBY

Is this the Cattleman's Suite?

HANNIBAL

Sure is. What can I do for you?

BOBBY

Are you alone?

HANNIBAL

No. Mr. McGruff, the hotel detective, is in the bedroom. Shall I get him for you?

BOBBY

No! Please…don't.

HANNIBAL

All right…as you like.

BOBBY

Say, how would you like to earn twenty dollars?

HANNIBAL

Twenty? I'm all ears!

(They hear McGRUFF coming.)

BOBBY

Quick! Hide me.

HANNIBAL

Back here.

(He motions toward the bar. BOBBY scurries around behind the bar and hides just as McGRUFF ENTERS from the bedroom.)

McGRUFF

Well that takes care of that.

(He checks the windows in the living area.)

I'll be off now. You've got your master key with you?

HANNIBAL

Yes, sir!

McGRUFF

Good. Keep a tight grip on it. Lock up when you finish with the bar. The occupants of this room are VIPs! They're presently at reception and they should be up shortly. I want you, moron, out of here before they arrive. Do you understand me?

HANNIBAL

As clear as rain water, sir!

McGRUFF

That's better. Trouble with young people today is they have no respect for their elders.

(He EXITS.)

HANNIBAL

He's gone...the idiot!

BOBBY

What was that all about?

HANNIBAL

That's Mr. McGruff. He thinks he owns the joint. He and Mr. Briar-butt are retired Navy officers. They forget that they're not in the service any longer. They think this hotel is a ship and we're all cadets or sailors or something. I tell you, this place is for the birds. What about the twenty dollars you spoke about?

BOBBY

Yeah, right. I need a little favor and I think an afternoon off would do you some good. You said you have a master key?

(HANNIBAL nods his head.)

That's wonderful!

(They hear voices in the hallway.)

They're coming. Is there another way out?

HANNIBAL

Sure. There's another door in the bedroom that leads to the hallway.

BOBBY

Great. Let's wait until they come in here and then we'll slip out the other door. There's a service room down the hallway, isn't there?

(HANNIBAL nods.)

Good. Let's talk there. Here's your twenty.

(He hands him a twenty-dollar bill as they slip off into the bedroom. The voices get louder. The hallway door opens. Enter BRIARBUSH, DRITH-ERS, and JULIE. McGRUFF follows carrying all the luggage. MARY ENTERS after McGRUFF.)

BRIARBUSH

So, my dearest Mr. Drithers, here we are at last. The Cattleman's Suite, as requested.

DRITHERS

This place sure brings back memories. Hasn't changed a bit. Just amazing.

McGRUFF

Sir...

(With heavy luggage in hand.)

BRIARBUSH

Don't interrupt.... We've taken the liberty to stock the wet bar with your favorite beverages...

McGRUFF

...Sir...

(Still holding the luggage.)

BRIARBUSH

Don't interrupt! Plus a few food items to curb your hunger. Please feel free to enjoy yourself at the bar; it's on the house...

DRITHERS

Well, thank you.

McGRUFF

...Sir!...

(Still holding the luggage.)

BRIARBUSH

Don't interrupt! You are so welcome! It's the greatest of pleasures to have you here with us again. And a great honor to host the engagement party of your most beautiful daughter.

JULIE

Thank you. Most kind indeed.

(McGRUFF sets the luggage down in the middle of the floor.)

BRIARBUSH

Don't just stand there McGruff, put their luggage in their bedrooms.

JULIE

These two are mine. I'll take them.

McGRUFF

Oh no, Miss Julie, I couldn't allow that.

JULIE

I insist!

BRIARBUSH

Your room is the east room, Miss. This direction, if you please. Let me help you with those things.

JULIE

Thank you, I can handle it just fine by myself.

BRIARBUSH

Very well, Miss Julie.

(McGRUFF is left with one piece of luggage—namely a very large and heavy travel locker—which he has carried on his back. Arching over, he picks it up on his back again and carries it into the stage left bedroom.)

DRITHERS

(Calling out.) Just set is down any old place. I'll do the unpacking myself. I don't want you messing with my rattlesnake.

(There is a yelp from McGRUFF in the bedroom.)

BRIARBUSH

It is such a pleasure to be able to provide for you for the few days you have chosen to be with us.

DRITHERS

Thank you.

BRIARBUSH

Allow me to introduce Mary. She is the maid responsible for your quarters.

(DRITHERS kisses her hand.)

If you have any needs whatsoever concerning the upkeep of your suite, please call upon Mary. She is available through the reception. Please dial 113 to reach the reception desk.

DRITHERS

Enchanted, my dear.

MARY

(Blushing.) Oh, Mr. Drithers.

BRIARBUSH

We've appointed a single bellboy to your room alone. You'll meet him shortly, I'm sure. His name is Hannibal. He'll be responsible for providing you with anything that you may need, apart from that which Mary will do for you. Room service, luggage, tobacco…

DRITHERS

Yes. How nice. I'm sure that Mary will be able to provide me with everything that I'll be needing. Such a lovely young lady.

MARY

(Blushing further.) Mr. Drithers!

DRITHERS

You're just as pretty as any filly I've seen in a month of Sundays.

MARY

You've gone an' embarrassed me now, Mr. Drithers, sir.

BRIARBUSH

So, Mr. Drithers, if I can be of any service to you, just let me know. This hotel could really use someone like you—someone whose leadership skills are so distinct, a man of courage and money...I mean...of monumental courage and...

DRITHERS

Well, thank you Mr. Briarbutt...

BRIARBUSH

Briarbush...bush...bush. Although, if you prefer...

DRITHERS

I am sorry. I was distracted, you understand.

(Looking in MARY'S direction.)

BRIARBUSH

Of course. No need for an apology.

DRITHERS

Thank you again. We'll manage just fine without you for a while. We'd like to be alone now.

(DRITHERS holds the door open. BRIARBUSH, McGRUFF, and MARY begin backing towards the hallway door.)

BRIARBUSH

Of course. That's only natural...after such a long journey from Houston...How is the weather in Houston?...and the oil wells?...I hear business is booming…ready to expand…perhaps ready to buy new holdings?…

DRITHERS

Go!!

(He slams the door in BRIARBUSH'S face.)

That Mr. Briarbutt is a real bush.

(He means "butt.")

JULIE

I thought they'd never leave. Are all the residents of Dallas so mangy, or just those two?

DRITHERS

Just those two prairie dogs. They both come from Oklahoma, no doubt. All the folks in Dallas are rich.

JULIE

I see. Daddy? Are you sure this is really the right thing? I mean, I'm only twenty-five. I don't really want to get married yet. I know how important it is for you and all, and I'd never want to disappoint you…

DRITHERS

Julie, dearest daughter. I promised your mother, God rest her soul, that I'd care for you and see that you married well. Marrying into a fine family like the Snooker's is just the thing that your mother would have wanted. And besides, they're like us—rich! That's important, too.

JULIE

I know that you and Mr. Snooker played football together at TDU and all, and that he's been your best friend ever since you can remember, but...his son is a bit of a geek.

DRITHERS

I think the word is "wallflower" dear.

JULIE

Call it what you will. Money or not, you could have picked a guy that had a little larger investment in the "handsome and good looking" bond market.

DRITHERS

Julie, think of your mother. We were engaged in this very room in just the same manner. Your mother didn't think much of my investment in the bond market either. But she married me all the same; knowing it to be the right thing to do. She never regretted her decision. She learned to love.

JULIE

That's the point. I do love somebody. I just didn't want to be married yet. I love Bobby. And I'd be happy to be his wife—in time. I just don't consider myself ready to marry.

DRITHERS

Julie. Dearest. Bobby is a pauper. I gave him a job because of you and because he's a nice fellow.

JULIE

But I want to marry for love.

DRITHERS

Your mother wouldn't approve. People don't marry for love. They marry for family and money and tradition. Enough now. Your mother is gonna be turning over in her grave, if she hears this. The engagement party is planned for tomorrow evening. I don't want to hear another word about Bobby. He's five hundred miles from here and has no business in your thoughts, or in your life for that matter. End of subject.

JULIE

Yes, Daddy. As you wish.

DRITHERS

Now. I'm going to freshen up and change clothes before lunch. I want to look my best when the Snookers arrive. They are long overdue.

JULIE

Yes, Daddy. I'll just sit here and read my magazine.

DRITHERS

If you get the chance, order us up some coffee, would you, dear? I could use a cup before lunch to get the old ticker going again.

(He EXITS to the stage left bedroom.)

JULIE

Sure, Daddy. I'll get to it in a while.

(There is a KNOCK at the door.)

Who's there?!

BOBBY

Room service!

JULIE

Go away! We didn't order anything!

BOBBY

(Knocking again.) Room service!

JULIE

Oh, go away, I said...

DRITHERS

(Off.) Who's at the door, Julie?

JULIE

A rather persistent bellboy. Did you order anything?

BOBBY

(Knocking again.) Room service!

DRITHERS

(Off.) No, but let's see what he's brought. It might be worth our while.

JULIE

It also might be another prairie dog from Oklahoma.

(DRITHERS ENTERS from the bedroom and moves to upstage center and opens the door. BOBBY stands outside with a service tray. He is dressed in a bellboy uniform. DRITHERS does not recognize him. JULIE has her back to the door and does not see him.)

DRITHERS

What is it?

BOBBY

Room service.

DRITHERS

I think we've caught on to that part.

BOBBY

Coffee for two.

DRITHERS

Now, that's what I call service! Put it on the table. Julie! Be a dear and give the boy a tip.

(He EXITS back to his bedroom.)

JULIE

Yes, Daddy.

BOBBY

Shall I put it here, Miss?

(He moves to the sofa table.)

JULIE

(She looks up and sees him.) Bobby?!

BOBBY

Keep it down! Do you want your father to hear?

JULIE

Bobby? What are you doing here?

BOBBY

I had to see you again.

JULIE

But why here? What about my father?

BOBBY

I don't care about him. It's you I love.

JULIE

Oh Bobby!

(They kiss.)

DRITHERS

(From the bedroom.) Did you find something to give the bellboy?

JULIE

Uh, yes, Daddy! I did!

(They kiss again.)

DRITHERS

Good. I hope you didn't give him too much. Over tipping will only make 'em greedy. Give 'em a hand and they'll take the whole arm!

JULIE

Yes, Daddy.

(They kiss passionately.)

DRITHERS

Don't pour the coffee just yet. I can't seem to get this damned tie to tie right. Without your mother to tie it for me, I'm afraid I'm just helpless. I much prefer my bolo tie to this noose contraption.

BOBBY

(Breaking the kiss.) Are you really going to marry that...that...

JULIE

Don't start with name calling. You know that he's the one Daddy's picked for me to marry...and...well...

BOBBY

But do you love him?

JULIE

Love him? I hardly know him! My heart belongs to you, Bobby. No matter who I marry, I'll always belong to you.

BOBBY

How can you let your father tell you who to marry?

JULIE

We've been through this before. He is just so insistent. I don't know how to tell him "no."

DRITHERS

(From the bedroom.) Julie dear. Who are you talking to?

JULIE

No one, Daddy! I'm just muttering to myself.

DRITHERS

Well, stop it. It's not attractive for the daughter of such a wealthy oilman like myself to be talking to herself, although I doubt you could find better company.

JULIE

(To BOBBY.) You've got to get out of here.

DRITHERS

(From the bedroom.) There. It took me an eternity, but the tie is finally on my neck.

JULIE

I'll hold him off. You disappear.

(She kisses him.)

I love you.

(She moves quickly to the bedroom and disappears. Voices heard in the outer hallway.)

BOBBY

And I love you, too.

(BOBBY scrambles to the front door, opens it to exit, but hears voices approaching in the hallway. He closes the door. He moves frantically about the room looking for a hiding place. He tries the window curtain routine and then the bar. He finally decides on the sofa. He crawls beneath the sofa just before DRITHERS ENTERS from the bedroom. JULIE follows him. The voices in the hallway grow louder.)

DRITHERS

...if you really think pink ties are unattractive for men, then why did you give me this one for my birthday last year?

JULIE

Oh, well...I...I didn't expect you to wear it. You never wore any of the other ties I gave you all the years before.

(JULIE searches the room with a glance and is satisfied that BOBBY made it out safely. There's a KNOCK at the door.)

DRITHERS

I always liked the ties you gave me. It's your mother who never let me wear them.

(*He moves to the door.*)

JULIE

That's strange. Mother always helped me pick them out.

DRITHERS

Well, let's see who's knocking at our door. It had better be ol' Snooker. He's more than an hour late as it is.

(*He opens the door. SNOOKER, SALLY and MATT are at the door.*)

Speak of the devil!

SNOOKER

Drithers, you ol' snake oil salesman!

(*They ENTER leaving the door open.*)

DRITHERS

Snooker, you ol' son-of-a-gun!

(*They exchange an exotic fraternity hand shake and a bear hug followed by their University battle cry…*)

TOGETHER

"Frog legs, frog legs, hop to the top. All the way to graduate, we're never gonna stop!"

(*They laugh.*)

DRITHERS

And Sally! You look just as pretty as ever! How long has it been? Ten? Fifteen years? Maybe longer?

SALLY

It's been two years. We saw each other at the college homecoming two years ago.

DRITHERS

I must have been too drunk to remember...

SALLY

That you were, Douglas B. Drithers. That you were.

DRITHERS

And this must be your son, Matthew?

SALLY

Well, it's not the bellboy! Who else should it be?

DRITHERS

Well, do come in and let's shut that door. It's a bit drafty with it open.

(They shut the door.)

SALLY

And you must be Douglas' daughter, Julie?

JULIE

Yes! A pleasure to make your acquaintance, Mrs. Snooker.

SALLY

You may call me Mom.

JULIE

Oh! What a surprise. Thank you…Mom.

SALLY

And you already know Matthew.

JULIE

Yes, of course. Hi, Matt.

MATT

Hello, Julie. You're looking really swell today.

JULIE

Thank you. Very kind of you to notice.

SALLY

I'm thrilled to see you and Matthew hit it off so well, so quickly. I knew this would be a marriage made in heaven.

DRITHERS

I know Julie's mother would be proud.

SALLY

Matthew has told me so much about you. Although he described you as beautiful, he didn't do you justice. You are a lovely girl. Don't you think so, Billows?

SNOOKER

Oh yes. An absolutely charming girl.

JULIE

Thank you...Mom...and Dad.

SNOOKER

Let's stick to Snooker, shall we.

JULIE

Right. Sorry.

SNOOKER

Not a problem. Just a preference. If my wife would only be so kind.

SALLY

Billows! That will be enough!

SNOOKER

Yes, dear.

SALLY

Matthew?! I think you still have something more to say, if I am not mistaken.

MATT

Yes, Mother.

SALLY

Well? Get on with it.

MATT

Yes, Mother dear. (*He clears his throat. He begins to recite.*) Mr. Drithers, sir. It will be the greatest of privileges to see our two families united through the common bonds of marriage. I express my deepest thanks for the opportunity to soon call you family. Although the arrangements have been made for us, I desire still to ask formally for your daughter's hand in marriage.

DRITHERS

Well, that's great. That really is wonderful of you. Isn't he something else, Snooker?

SNOOKER

He sure is!

DRITHERS

Well? Go ahead.

MATT

Go ahead what?

DRITHERS

You said you wanted to ask me for my daughter's hand in marriage. So go ahead.

MATT

Oh! I thought...Oh right! Now I get it. Mr. Drithers, sir. May I have your daughter's hand in marriage?

DRITHERS

Why, of course. That's what this whole thing's about!

MATT

Why...that's just wonderful!

DRITHERS

A good boy you have here, Snook!

SNOOKER

Thanks. He takes after my wife's side of the family.

SALLY

Enough now, Billows!

SNOOKER

Yes dear.

SALLY

Matthew, dear. I think you have something else to say.

MATT

Yes, mother. I got a little sidetracked. Sorry. *(He clears his throat again and recites.)* Dearest Julie, I am ever so thankful to have made your acquaintance. Your beauty is a treasure I do not deserve…

SALLY

That is, of course, a matter of opinion. Nothing is too good for my little Matthew.

SNOOKER

Sally! Don't interrupt. You know how hard it is for him to find his place again.

SALLY

Sorry. Please continue Matthew.

(He repeats to himself the part he has already recited. When he gets to the point where he left off, he continues aloud.)

MATT

Your eyes are like pools of saffires. Your skin is milky white like the pearls of the oyster fair. Your…Your…ears are covered by your hair so…clean…

JULIE

Thank you Matt. That is really plenty; and really sweet of you, too. But let's not ruin it on the first day. What do you say? Maybe tomorrow?

MATT

Alright. If you want.

SALLY

That was wonderful, Matthew. He has such a deep inner need to express himself with poetry.

MATT

I also like to compose songs.

JULIE

I think I'm going to be sick.

SNOOKER

Speaking of deep inner needs, I'm getting hungry.

DRITHERS

I'm sure you are not the only one, Snooker, old pal. Julie, dearest. If you would be so kind and take our guests down to the bar for a drink. Snooker and I will join you in the restaurant in about twenty minutes.

JULIE

Very well. Did you remember to make a reservation?

DRITHERS

Of course. A table for five with a view of the city. Reserved for twelve-thirty. If ya'll don't hurry along now, we're going miss our table.

SNOOKER

Go along with Julie, my dears. We'll be down in a few minutes. We need to talk business before we sit down to lunch.

SALLY

Yes, dear.

(SALLY, MATT and JULIE EXIT.)

DRITHERS

You old web foot, it's good to see you again.

SNOOKER

Once a web foot, always a web foot! Matt will be graduating from TDU next month. I can't say how proud I am that he's chosen to walk in my footsteps, as I walked in my father's footsteps, as did...

DRITHERS

...his father before him. Yes, yes. It's the same here. Since Julie's mother died, I have tried to provide for her the best way I could. I was so proud when she graduated from TDU three years ago. But can you imagine, four years at that school and never met a man she could marry?! Her mother went to TDU just for that purpose—to find a husband! She studied three semesters and then quit once she found me. She got what she came for—and I don't mean an education.

SNOOKER

The youth of today just aren't the same as they were when we were young.

DRITHERS

Well, it looks like her holding-off with a husband is working out to our advantage. The thought of such a "merger"—your family and mine!

SNOOKER

Your company and mine!

DRITHERS

Your fortune and mine!

SNOOKER

Your debts and mine…

DRITHERS

Come on, Snook! Let's not kid ourselves. If our companies don't merge together this year, we will both be broke by Christmas.

SNOOKER

Think of the headlines! "Spectacular Wedding of Industrial Wizard's Son with Oilman's Daughter," followed by "Company's Assets Bequeathed to Daughter as Oilman Retires."

DRITHERS

"Major Merger Awaits Newlyweds."

SNOOKER

And best of all…"Oil Company Stocks Triple Overnight."

DRITHERS

If we pull it off, we'll be saved from ruin and bankruptcy!

SNOOKER

We can retire early and live in luxury, knowing our families are provided for. Happy end!

DRITHERS

Are you sure your son is ready for this?

SNOOKER

He's putty in my hand! The moron has no brain of his own; not yet anyway. He'll do exactly as I say. Besides, he thinks your daughter is the prettiest thing he's ever seen. He's absolutely crazy for her. And what about your daughter?

DRITHERS

Julie? Oh, she's fine. She'll do whatever I tell her to do. She's easily manipulated. She had four years to marry some "frog" and blew it. I don't feel bad about it at all. Considering what we will lose if we don't marry the two kids off soon, I would feel worse if we didn't do it. Once they get used to the idea, they'll be fine. As long as that romantic jackass, Bobby, stays away, we should be okay.

SNOOKER

Who's Bobby?

DRITHERS

An old boyfriend. He seems to have an unusual influence on her. I hired him in the company and then sent him to El Paso to work. That way, he was far away from Julie. After that, she became the good old "putty-in-my-hand" that she's always been. So long as he doesn't show up at the engagement party, we should be in the clear.

SNOOKER

Fine! Hey, since we're missing happy hour, let me propose a toast!

DRITHERS

With what? Cold coffee? Let me get something from the bar.

SNOOKER

Drithers, you old fool! You know me better that that. I never travel unprepared.

(He lifts his trouser leg and unsnaps a bootleg flask from his leg. He unscrews the cap and holds up the flask.)

To the enlargement of our families and their holdings.

(He drinks and hands the flask to DRITHERS.)

DRITHERS

To Julie and to Matt.

BOTH

And to our retirement!

(They laugh. DRITHERS drinks and returns the flask to SNOOKER.)

SNOOKER

Come now, let's be off before Sally sends the hotel detective up to find us!

DRITHERS.

She never changes, does she?

(They laugh as they EXIT. BOBBY squeezes out from under the sofa. Exhausted from hiding, angry at what he has heard. He sits on the sofa.)

BOBBY

A romantic jackass, am I? We'll just see about that!

(He moves to the telephone and dials.)

Hello, room service? Yes. I would like to order a dozen red roses please. No, make that two-dozen. *(Pause.)* Yes. Deliver them today please to Miss Julie Drithers on the thirteenth floor, room 1310. And please attach a card to it. The card should read "from a secret admirer." That's correct. And charge it to Drithers Oil Incorporated. Yes, thank you very much.

(He hangs up.)

Fear not, Julie. Your romantic jackass won't let you down!

(He moves upstage center and EXITS as lights fade.)

BLACKOUT

SCENE 2

Two hours later, about 1:30 p.m. At LIGHTS UP, we hear a key rattle in the lock of the hallway door. DRITHERS ENTERS. He is returning from a big lunch. A toothpick hangs from his mouth. He goes to his bedroom and returns immediately with his briefcase. He opens it at the bar and confirms that his papers are in order. He closes the briefcase and moves towards the hallway door to leave. He does a double take at the bar and returns to fix himself a drink. As he does, there is a KNOCK at the door. He calls out.

DRITHERS

Who is it?!

MARY

Room service!

DRITHERS

One moment.

(He finishes fixing his drink and then moves to the door with glass in hand. He opens the door.)

Yes, what is it?

MARY

Afternoon, sir. I have an order of roses to deliver. May I come in?

DRITHERS.

Of course. Come in…come in. Mary, wasn't it?

MARY

Yes sir, how kind of you to remember.

(She rolls her service cart with the flowers into the room.)

DRITHERS

How could I forget? Someone so attractive as yourself.

MARY

Oh, Mr. Drithers, sir! You embarrass me. Shall I put the flowers here, sir?

DRITHERS.

That'll be fine. Tell me, Mary…would you like to stay and have a drink with me? I have a business meeting to attend with my new partner, but I could put it off for a while.

MARY

Oh no, sir! I'll be going now. I've lots to be doing. And I'm sure Mr. Briarbush wouldn't approve. Thank you for the offer. Most kind, sir.

(She rolls her cart to the hallway door and EXITS.)

DRITHERS

Too bad. So! Who is sending whom flowers.

(He moves to the table, sets down his drink, and looks for a card. Finding it, he opens it and reads it.)

"To Julie. The woman of my dreams. From a secret admirer." What the devil…Now I wonder…No, he's in El Paso and hasn't heard about all this yet…and Matthew is too much of a blockhead to send flowers, let alone pretend to be a secret anything. Well, we'll just fix this right now.

(He pulls a pen from his coat and looks through his briefcase for a card. He then writes.)

"To Julie. My bride to be. From Matthew." There!

(He places the card in the roses again. He laughs as he moves to the bar.)

I hope Mr. secret admirer doesn't mind picking up the bill for Matthew's gift of roses.

(He chuckles as he gets his briefcase and his drink and EXITS out the hallway door. There are a few moments of silence. We then hear a KNOCK and then a key in the lock of the hallway door. The door opens slowly. We see JASPER and FRANK, two men in their forties, ENTER the room.)

JASPER

Hello?! Anyone home? Room service here. Hello? Looks like the coast is clear, Frank.

FRANK

Well? We're in. What now, Jasper?

JASPER

First, we keep the noise down. We don't want to draw any attention to ourselves. Second, we case the joint. Mr. Warner from the Dallas Regency Hotel said to do whatever we had to do to make this hotel look bad. He left the "what and how" up to us. He simply said, spread some mud about and don't leave any trail for the cops to follow. It should just look like hotel employee incompetence. If we do our job well, we get paid a big bonus. If not?

(He gestures his throat being cut.)

So look about and see what might lend itself to our cause. Start in there, all right? And hold the noise down.

FRANK

All right!

(A beat.)

Hey, what about short sheeting old Mr. Drithers and putting some itching powder in the girl's bed?

JASPER

Be a little more creative, would you!

FRANK

We could water down the booze!

(JASPER glares at him.)

Or how about putting molasses on the door handles and butter on the toilet seat?!

JASPER

Too obvious. If we're to get our bonus, it's got to look natural; not like summer camp pranks. Besides, one trick like that and they'd be on us in a moment.

FRANK

Well, have you got any ideas, Mr. Genius, sir?!

JASPER

Hey, what do we have here?!

FRANK

Looks like flowers to me.

JASPER

Thanks for the insight, Professor. Of course they're flowers. Listen to this.

(He reads.)

"To Julie. My bride to be. From Matthew."

FRANK

That's sweet.

JASPER

That's it. Quick give me a pen. I think we have the perfect trick.

(He digs for a card or paper and begins to write.)

"To Julie. The woman of my dreams. From a secret admirer." There! That should turn the heat up on the engagement party.

FRANK

That's great, boss! I wish I could be around to see her face...

JASPER

Better yet, the look on old Drithers' face!

(They laugh.)

All right now. One last piece of business. Let's go downstairs and keep an eye on Drithers. When he's back in the room, we'll give him a ring from the lobby and pretend to be from the local paper. We will tell him we've been given an anonymous tip from the hotel staff that Miss Julie has a secret admirer. He'll blow up right then and there! He'll go looking for Briarface and give it to him with both barrels!

(They laugh.)

FRANK

You're good, boss. Really good.

JASPER

Thanks. I sometimes surprise myself. Come on. Let's get out of here before they come back.

(They hear noises outside in the hallway.)

FRANK

Too late. What'll we do?

JASPER

In here. There's bound to be another way out.

(They EXIT to the stage left bedroom. The voices in the hallway get louder. As JULIE and DRITHERS ENTER through the hallway door, JASPER and FRANK EXIT out the bedroom hallway door.)

JULIE

Really, Daddy. I wish you wouldn't flirt with the hired help that way. Those young girls have jobs to do and all your attentions only make it more difficult.

DRITHERS

They never complain.

JULIE

Of course not. If one of those girls hauled off and slapped you, she'd be out of work tomorrow.

DRITHERS

I'm only having a little fun. There's nothing meant by it at all.

JULIE

Hey, look! Roses!

(She moves to the table.)

DRITHERS

Oh yeah, I forget to mention it earlier. The maid delivered them after lunch when I was up getting my papers.

JULIE

Oh, they're beautiful. Here's a card. Let's see who has been so thoughtful.

(She reads.) "To Julie. The woman of my dreams. From a secret admirer."

DRITHERS

What?!!

JULIE

How exciting!

DRITHERS

It says what?!!

JULIE

That's right! "From a secret admirer." How romantic!

DRITHERS

Romantic? Nonsense. I'm sure Matthew sent them. He has a funny sense of humor, that's all. Let me see that.

(He takes the card from JULIE and reads it silently.)

Now that's strange.

(He digs in the trashcan. He finds the card he wrote, which was discarded by Jasper, and reads it aloud.)

"My bride to be. Matthew." I must have thrown away the wrong card. Strange?

JULIE

What's that Daddy?

DRITHERS

Nothing dear. Just talking to myself.

JULIE

It's not right that a rich oilman like yourself should be talking to himself...although you probably won't find better company.

(She smiles at him, but he is too deep in thought to respond. The PHONE RINGS. JULIE is teeming with delight over her roses and secret admirer.)

DRITHERS

I'll get it.

(He moves to the phone.)

Hello. Yes, this is Douglas B. Drithers. *(Pause.)* Well, yes. Hello. *(To JULIE.)* It's the newspaper! *(Continuing.)* No! I'm not willing to make a statement about my daughter's upcoming engagement plans. That'll all be made clear at the engagement party tomorrow night...not a word until then. *(Pause.)* You've heard what?!!...No it's not true. You've heard wrong! Goodbye! *(He hangs up.)* The nerve of that guy!

JULIE

What was that about?

DRITHERS

The newspaper received an anonymous tip from someone among the hotel staff that you have a secret admirer.

JULIE

News travels fast.

DRITHERS

No, it doesn't. Those flowers are from Matthew B. Snooker. I'm going to find Mr. Briarbutt...

JULIE

...bush...

DRITHERS

...and give him a piece of my mind. After that, we're going to pay a visit to the Snookers and you'll see that I'm right. Secret admirer? Blah!

(He moves to the hallway door.)

JULIE

...but Daddy?!...

(He EXITS.)

Is it really so important?

(She moves to the flowers and smells them. She thinks about Bobby. There is a KNOCK at the door.)

Yes, who's there?

BOBBY

Room service!

(JULIE dashes to the door.)

JULIE

(Through the door, quietly.) Bobby?

BOBBY

Yes, it's me.

(She opens the door and BOBBY ENTERS.)

JULIE

Oh, Bobby!

(They hug.)

BOBBY

I passed your Father in the hallway. How long will he be gone for?

JULIE

Five minutes, maybe. Did he see you?!

BOBBY

He saw me, sure, but he didn't recognize me.

JULIE

Oh, Bobby.

(They kiss.)

Did you send me the roses?

BOBBY

Yes, of course.

JULIE

Daddy insisted that Matt sent them. What are you doing here in Dallas, anyway? I thought you were supposed to be in El Paso.

BOBBY

I was sent by the company to deliver an important letter to Mr. Drithers. They tried to reach him by phone, but he had already left for Dallas. The branch manager didn't want to wait for the mail, the news being urgent, so they sent me—à la pony express! But when I got to the hotel and discovered the announcement of your engagement party, I flipped out. I figured the letter delivery could wait.

JULIE

Oh, Bobby! I love you.

(They kiss.)

BOBBY

Julie. You can't marry Matt.

JULIE

Bobby, we've been through this all before. It's what Daddy wants!

BOBBY

You don't understand. When I was here last, I didn't make it out of the room before the Snookers showed up.

JULIE

Oh?

BOBBY

I hid under the sofa instead. After you left with Matt and Mrs. Snooker to go downstairs, Snooker and your Father talked about the wedding plans and their business deals.

JULIE

What does that have to do with me?

BOBBY

The only reason that your father wants you to marry Snooker's son is for profit. Your father is broke! So is Snooker. They're trying to use the wedding to boost confidence in their companies. Their plan is to merge the two companies before the end of the year. They each own the lion's share of stock in their own companies. If the price per share of stock skyrockets after the marriage/merger, they'll both be millionaires again. I tell you, Julie, you're just a pawn on your father's chessboard. Just one more asset.

JULIE

Oh daddy! How could you?

(She starts to cry. BOBBY holds her.)

Are you sure you heard them right? You wouldn't just say that to try and stop the engagement, would you?

BOBBY

Never! I love you, Julie.

(They kiss.)

JULIE

What are we to do?!

BOBBY

I'm not sure yet. Give me a while to work out a plan. Until then, don't let on that you know what's going on. Drag your feet all you can.

JULIE

Bobby, dearest. Don't let me down. I've always been ready to do whatever Daddy wanted, but this is going too far. I'm his daughter, not an oil well!

(Noises in the hallway. They kiss quickly and BOBBY dives under the sofa. A key is heard in the lock and the door opens. DRITHERS ENTERS. He is still very angry.)

DRITHERS

I looked everywhere. No one seems to know where he is. I think he caught wind that I was looking for him. Just as well. I might do more than just hog tie him, as mad as I am right now. I might just hang him from the top of one of my oil wells.

JULIE

Speaking of oil wells, Daddy. How's the business going?

DRITHERS

Fine. Just fine. I think I need a drink.

(He moves to the bar.)

JULIE

I thought you had trouble in drilling?

DRITHERS

Drilling? Huh?

(Fixes drink.)

JULIE

You told me a couple of weeks ago that the company hadn't been successful with finding new wells and that the old wells were starting to dry up!

DRITHERS

I said that?

(She nods.)

Well? What of it? We've plenty of reserves to hold us over until we hit pay dirt again. Enough of this.

JULIE

I was just curious. If you want, we can talk about something else like flowers. I wonder what handsome lover might be out there admiring me from afar?

DRITHERS

Enough of that, as well. Those roses are from Matthew B. Snooker. To prove it, we're going straight over to Snookers' suite and ask Matthew about it. Come along now. You'll see directly. March!

(They EXIT. BOBBY crawls out from under the sofa and sits on the sofa.)

BOBBY

That girl's got spunk. Well!

(Takes envelope from his pocket.)

I wonder what was so almighty important that they had to send it special delivery. Well, let's just see.

(He opens the envelope and reads, silently at first…)

…"We tried to reach you in Houston, but you were already gone…knowing how important…we knew you would want to know without delay…We struck oil on the Johnson property…It looks like the biggest strike since thirty-six…"

(He hears noises in the hallway. He folds the letter and puts it in his pocket. He crawls quickly under the sofa again. There is a KNOCK at the door. And then another. A moment later there is a key rattling in the hallway door and it opens. JASPER and FRANK ENTER. They are dressed as bellboys. They are pushing a maid's laundry service cart.)

JASPER

Hello? Room service.

(Pause.)

Just as we thought. The place is empty.

FRANK

The look on Drithers' face when he was storming through the lobby was unbelievable. Have you ever seen anyone so mad in all your life?

JASPER

It's what makes this line of work so attractive.

FRANK

These uniforms are a great idea. We can come and go at will and nobody ever asks a question.

JASPER

It's called "traveling incognito."

FRANK

I find it "neat-o" too, boss.

JASPER

Never mind.

FRANK

So, what's next, Jasper?

JASPER

Next, we must somehow pin this secret lover bit on the hotel staff. My plan runs like this: I'm a bellboy, see? I'll stay here and hit up on the girl when she returns. I'll hide in her bedroom, you see. When she comes in, I'll tell her the flowers were from me and that I love her and want her, right? When she's had enough, I'll escape and disappear. She'll tell Daddy and Daddy will take Briarface apart piece by piece.

FRANK

That's a super idea! And what'll I be doing the whole time?

JASPER

You're gonna go downstairs and find a gullible member of the hotel's cleaning staff and spread a rumor that old Mr. Drithers is rushing little Miss Julie's engagement because she's expecting.

FRANK

Expecting what?

JASPER

A baby, stupid. A baby! You're gonna spread the rumor that Miss Julie is pregnant. Get it?

FRANK

What? She's pregnant? So that's why she's in such a hurry to get married.

JASPER

No, no, no. She's not pregnant. But you're gonna spread the rumor that she is. It won't take long for it to get back to Drithers. Once he gets wind that the hotel staff has been spreading the nasty rumors, he'll have the whole company in court before the week is out!

FRANK

I see now! That's brilliant. But why can't I stay and put the make on the girl. You always get the good jobs.

JASPER

That's because I'm the brains in this outfit. Got it?!

FRANK

But you don't need any brains to put the make on a girl...

JASPER

You do what I say or you won't get paid! Got it now?!

FRANK

Right boss! You put the make on the girl and I'll go and spread the nasty rumors. Right!

JASPER

Enough now. Get downstairs now and find yourself a pigeon. I'll get a feel for the suite until the girl shows up.

FRANK

Right.

JASPER

When I finish up here, I'll meet you in the storage room behind the kitchen.

FRANK

Right.

(FRANK EXITS upstage center. JASPER moves to JULIE'S bedroom and disappears from view. BOBBY crawls out from under the sofa and moves to behind the bar. He's looking for a makeshift weapon. He crouches down behind the bar as he hears Jasper coming. JASPER ENTERS and moves to DRITHERS' bedroom. He disappears from view. BOBBY continues his search for a weapon. He holds up various bar items and bottles. He finally

settles on the silver champagne stand. There are noises in the bedroom toilet. The sound of a toilet flushing offstage left. BOBBY quickly moves around to stageleft of the bar and crouches down out of sight of the bedroom door. JASPER ENTERS from the bedroom. He stops in front of the bar. He decides to make himself a drink and moves around behind the bar. He bends over, out of sight, to search the liquor supply. As he does, BOBBY stands and leans over the bar. He raises the champagne stand above his head and, using it as a club, hits JASPER over the head. We hear JASPER'S body fall unconscious to the floor behind the bar. BOBBY wipes his brow and moves around behind the bar. He drags the unconscious JASPER to JULIE'S bedroom and dumps him in JULIE'S bed. He returns to the bar to clean up his mess. As he finishes, he hears noises in the hallway. He dives under the sofa as he hears a key in the lock. The door opens. JULIE ENTERS. She is alone. She is upset. She crosses to her room and disappears from view. She screams and runs from the room using the upstage center door. BOBBY crawls out from under the sofa and EXITS into JULIE'S bedroom. He drags JASPER to the sofa and shoves him under the sofa. He hears footsteps in the hallway. He looks for a new hiding place. Seeing the maid's service cart that FRANK and JASPER brought with them, he crawls into the laundry bag. He pulls the sheets over his head just as JULIE, DRITHERS, who carries a briefcase, SNOOKER, McGRUFF, BRIARBUSH and MARY ENTER the room. DRITHERS sets his briefcase down near the upstage center door as he ENTERS. JULIE runs to her bedroom doorway and points inside.)

JULIE

In there! There's a body in my bed!!

McGRUFF

Dead or alive, Miss?

JULIE

I don't know. I didn't stop to ask him.

(DRITHERS, McGRUFF and BRIARBUSH EXIT into the bedroom. They return with confused looks on their faces.)

DRITHERS

Julie, dearest. There isn't a body in your bed.

BRIARBUSH

Nor is there a body in your bedroom at all.

JULIE

But there has to be! It was there just a minute ago. Really!

McGRUFF

What did the body look like?

JULIE

It was red.

BRIARBUSH

Red?

JULIE

I mean it was wearing red. A bellboy. It was a bellboy. He was laying there on top of my bed like he was dead or unconscious.

DRITHERS

Mr. Briarbutt…

BRIARBUSH

...bush...

DRITHERS

...I don't know what's going on here, but if your bellboys are taking liberties...

BRIARBUSH

I assure you, Mr. Drithers, sir, that our bellboys are above such reproach...

DRITHERS

What's that?

(Pointing to the maid's service cart.)

BRIARBUSH

What's what?

DRITHERS

That!

BRIARBUSH

It's a hotel service cart.

DRITHERS

I know that. What is it doing in our room? It wasn't here earlier.

(JULIE moves to the sofa and sits. She notices an arm sticking out from under the sofa. She assumes it to be BOBBY'S arm. During the next por-

tion of dialogue, she attempts to push the arm back under the sofa. As she does, a leg pops out instead. This goes on for a while. She attempts discretion, not wanting to draw attention to herself or the person under the sofa. She does not want to give BOBBY'S hiding place away. In the end she sits on the floor with her back to the sofa and covers the arm with the sofa pillows.)

McGRUFF

It seems somebody was here after all. I think we can assume someone came to change the sheets and simply fell asleep while doing the job. Maybe the person wasn't well and simply fainted. Your scream, Miss, surely awakened the fellow and he left the room in a hurry.

DRITHERS

That's a plausible explanation, McGruff, but not a satisfactory one.

BRIARBUSH

I am so sorry, sir. We'll do a full investigation of the incident and find who is to blame for the matter. Mary! Get this cart out of here.

MARY

Yes, Mr. Briarbush, sir.

(MARY EXITS upstage center with the cart and BOBBY hiding under the laundry.)

BRIARBUSH

Again, I am so sorry. If we can do anything...

DRITHERS

You can see that we're not disturbed again.

BRIARBUSH

Right! You can count on us. McGruff! I want a full investigation and I want you to start on it this very minute!

McGRUFF

Yes sir! Right away, sir!

(He EXITS upstage center.)

BRIARBUSH

Let me express again, sir…

DRITHERS

Get out!

BRIARBUSH

Right! Right away! Thank you, sir!

(He EXITS upstage center.)

DRITHERS

Julie? Are you gonna be all right?

JULIE

Yes, Daddy. I just want to be left alone, that's all.

DRITHERS

Very well. I'll be in Snooker's suite again, if you need me.

JULIE

Thanks.

(DRITHERS jabs SNOOKER in the arm, giving him the "high sign" to say something.)

SNOOKER

Huh? Oh, yeah. Right. Julie. I am sorry about the roses. We didn't mean to upset you with the card. If it makes things any better, it was all my idea. I wanted to bring a little excitement to the engagement, you understand.

JULIE

Thank you, Mr. Snooker. I assure you, I understand fully. May I please be alone now?

SNOOKER

Yes. Yes, of course.

DRITHERS

Come now.

(The two men EXIT upstage center, but leave the door ajar. DRITHERS has left his briefcase on the floor near the door. JULIE sighs. She removes the pillows covering JASPER'S arm. She embraces the arm, holding the hand near to her heart.)

JULIE

They're gone now, Bobby. I thought they'd never leave. We're alone now...Just you and me...How romantic it is to have my secret admirer hiding under the sofa...taking such risks...all because of a burning passion to see me!...Oh Bobby! I love you, too!...and, although I may be married to another man, my heart belongs to no one else but you...Although I am embarrassed to talk about it, I wish my body belonged to you, too...Not just my heart...Oh Bobby, my one true love, I often imagined what it would be like with you on our honeymoon, if Daddy would have ever approved of our marriage. Shall I tell you about it.

(There is a groan from under the sofa. JASPER is slowly coming around. As she talks, DRITHERS ENTERS through the upstage center door, which Snooker left ajar. JULIE does not notice him. DRITHERS moves only three steps into the room. He is looking for his briefcase. He stops when he hears JULIE'S "love talk.")

JULIE

(Continuing.) I was lying there in our bed. I was dressed only in my lacy negligee. Oh Bobby! How exciting it was, to see you there, standing above me, ready to have me. You placed your strong right arm behind my neck as you embraced me and kissed me. With your other hand you disrobed me.

(DRITHERS registers shock and tiptoes quietly out of the door with briefcase in hand.)

With eyes of passion and fire burning in your soul, you told me of your love for me...

(There is another groan from under the sofa.)

Oh yes, Bobby, yes. Then...then...you kissed me with the passion of a thousand kisses held prisoner by the walls of propriety. My heart melted within my breast and I remembered no more...Oh Bobby, my love...kiss me...kiss me...

(She pushes the sofa backwards to reveal her lover. When she sees the only partially conscious JASPER again, she screams and runs from the room. As she EXITS the room, she moves down the hallway stageright, leaving the door open. JASPER gets up. Rubbing his head, he EXITS down the hallway in the opposite direction. He also leaves the door open. We hear footsteps and voices. JULIE appears again with DRITHERS, BRIAR-BUSH, McGRUFF and MARY.)

JULIE

There!! Under the sofa! He was under the sofa.

(She stands stage center as DRITHERS inspects the sofa.)

DRITHERS

Well, he's not there now. Mr. Briarbutt...

BRIARBUSH

...bush...

DRITHERS

...this is getting out of hand. If this kind of nonsense happens tomorrow evening at the engagement party, I will have your head on a platter. Do you hear me?!

(During the following dialogue, MARY circles around JULIE staring at her waist. When she completes the circle, she curtsies and EXITS upstage center.)

BRIARBUSH

Oh yes sir! Again, let me express my deepest apologies for these most embarrassing incidents. If you'll give us just two more hours, we'll get to the bottom of this whole thing. It does take time to find the old needle-in-the-haystack, you understand...

(He stops abruptly when he notices MARY'S business. She uses the break in dialogue for her exit. McGRUFF picks up the story after MARY'S EXIT.)

McGRUFF

Exactly! Mr. Drithers, sir. We've never had a problem like this before. This hotel has always had the most courteous staff that one could imagine. Although mistakes are made and things do go wrong, there is nothing that we won't do to make it right again. Please give us a chance, sir. I remember in 1938 when one of our guests was accidentally doused with gasoline. Why the entire staff of the hotel volunteered to stop smoking for a whole week.

(SALLY ENTERS upstage center. During McGRUFF'S dialogue, she circles around JULIE staring at her waist. When she completes the circle, she displays embarrassment and EXITS upstage center.)

That's right. We couldn't undo the damage, but we sure could try and set it right.

(He stops abruptly when he notices SALLY. She uses the break in dialogue for her EXIT.)

JULIE

What is going on here? Am I a part of a fashion show that no one's told me about? Enough! I'm going to change into my bathing suit and go downstairs for a swim. I've had enough for one day.

(She EXITS to her bedroom downstage right.)

DRITHERS

Have you made the arrangements for the engagement party as I requested?

BRIARBUSH

Oh yes sir, of course, sir. The cleaning staff arrives at four o'clock to set the room straight. The buffet tables will be here half-past five. The hors-d'œuvres and other eatables will be sent up at six o'clock. The bar will be stocked before half-past six. You can expect all the service personnel to arrive at a quarter-'til-seven.

DRITHERS

And the champagne? Did the champagne arrive yet?

BRAIRBUSH

Oh yes, sir! It arrived this morning, all the way from Paris, France. We have laid it on ice already. It will be served cold in crystal glasses, just as you prescribed, sir. There is nothing too good for Drithers Oil Incorporated, is there, sir?

DRITHERS

Just make sure the hired help don't help themselves to the champagne. I'm paying eighty-nine dollars per bottle for that Champagne and I'm not having your bellboys get drunk on my tab. Do I make myself clear?!

BRIARBUSH

Oh yes, sir. Very clear. You can depend upon us!

DRITHERS

If there's nothing else, gentlemen, I think you can be getting on with it.

BRIARBUSH

Right! Thank you, sir! It is such a pleasure and privilege to have you here at the Dallas Grand Hotel. You won't regret your choice. We'll give you the absolute grandest engagement party that anyone has ever seen.

DRITHERS

Go!

BRIARBUSH

Right! Go. Right. McGruff! Let's be going. Can't you see that Mr. Drithers wants to be left in peace. Don't dawdle. Get going...

(SNOOKER ENTERS upstage center as BRIARBUSH and McGRUFF EXIT. JULIE ENTERS from her bedroom downstage right. She moves to stage center. She is wearing a bathrobe over her bathing suit. Under her robe and around her waist she wears a towel. As SNOOKER ENTERS, she closes the robe, thus hiding the towel.)

JULIE

Are they finally gone? Oh, Mr. Snooker? Hi.

DRITHERS

Hi, Snooker.

SNOOKER

Hello.

JULIE

Well, you two enjoy yourselves. I'm going for a swim.

(SNOOKER is acting a little strange. He too circles around JULIE in amazement.)

Has the whole world gone mad? I'm going swimming now. If I may? At least by the pool there will be fewer people to gawk at me than up here.

(She EXITS upstage center.)

DRITHERS

Would you like to tell me what's going on here? You're the third person in the last half-hour to give Julie the old once over.

SNOOKER

Old friend, we need to talk. An engagement might not be just the right thing after all.

DRITHERS

Snooker! What in tarnation are you talking about?

SNOOKER

I'm not sure how to tell you this, so I'll just have to be blunt about it. You see,…well…Julie is…and well…Matt isn't…and that's about as clear as I can make it…and well, with those flowers and lover and all…

DRITHERS

Snook, old boy! What are you trying to say?

SNOOKER

Julie's pregnant!

DRITHERS

Pregnant? Julie? And Matt isn't the...

(SNOOKER shakes his head "no" in answer to DRITHERS' unfinished question. DRITHERS looks shocked. He glances to the sofa, then to SNOOKER, then back to the sofa. He looks faint.)

DRITHERS

I think I need a drink.

SNOOKER

A double?

DRITHERS

The bottle!

BLACKOUT

Act Two

SCENE 1

The next day at half-past six o'clock. The engagement party is scheduled to begin in thirty minutes. The suite is now decorated and arranged for the engagement party. There is a buffet table prepared and there are party decorations. The bar is stocked for a party, as well. JULIE is in her bedroom dressing. DRITHERS is on a bar stool drinking. He has been drinking for a while. There is KNOCK at the door.

DRITHERS

The door's open.

(The door opens and SNOOKER ENTERS.)

Oh, it's you. Do you want a drink?

SNOOKER

Have you talked to her about it, yet?

DRITHERS

No.

SNOOKER

Then I'll have a double!

DRITHERS

Then fix it yourself!

(SNOOKER moves to behind the bar and fixes himself a scotch.)

SNOOKER

Fine. Douglas, old friend, you've had more than twenty-four hours to ask her about it. What's the hold up?!

DRITHERS

She was asleep.

SNOOKER

Not for the whole day!

DRITHERS

I didn't dare bring it up last night. I was too angry to talk about it. Then she was asleep. Then I had breakfast. I couldn't bring it up at breakfast without ruining her appetite.

SNOOKER

I'm surprised you found any appetite yourself for breakfast after staying up the whole night.

DRITHERS

One doesn't need an appetite to digest a double whiskey sour.

SNOOKER

…for breakfast?

DRITHERS

Do you have any better suggestions?

SNOOKER

Yes. Talk with her. You can't just marry her off when she's expecting somebody else's baby! Talk with her. Find out whose baby it is. Then, at least, you can put your shotgun to work to make this whole thing right.

DRITHERS

I think I know who the father is.

SNOOKER

Yeah?…but you're just guessing.

DRITHERS

No. You see, I overheard Julie talking to herself…Yesterday, when I came back to get my briefcase…She was here talking out loud about her…liaison with Bobby and how she regrets having to marry another…

SNOOKER

No!?…and she didn't see you?

DRITHERS

No. The door was ajar. I just took my briefcase and backed quietly out of the room. I didn't want to make much of it…I mean, kids will be kids, but I never dreamed that she'd be pregnant.

SNOOKER

What a mess. You have got to talk to her. Right now! The engagement party is scheduled to begin in less than a half hour. We can't announce an engagement, if there's not going to be a wedding.

DRITHERS

I've already handled that. I've instructed Briarbutt to have the invited guests met in the lobby. They'll be escorted to the bar or restaurant. They can eat and drink on my tab 'til they're sick. I'll show up later to explain the whole thing and send them on their way.

SNOOKER

Clever idea. The last thing we need is all the society snobs messing in our private business.

(They drink.)

Where's she at, Doug?

DRITHERS

In her bedroom, changing.

SNOOKER

Talk to her!

DRITHERS.

All right, all right. I'll do it.

(He downs the drink.)

SNOOKER

…and be kind with her. She may have made a mistake, but she's still your only daughter.

DRITHERS

Right. Her mother is surely turning over in her grave, but she is still my only offspring. Why couldn't she have been a boy, instead? This kind of thing is considered okay when a young man does it, oh, but woe to the parents of the young lady!

SNOOKER

Go!

DRITHERS

All right. I'm going…I'm going.

(He moves downstage right to JULIE'S bedroom door. He hesitates for a moment, then, taking a deep breath, he raises his hand to KNOCK. At the same moment, there is a KNOCK at the front door upstage center. DRITHERS feels as if he has been "saved by the bell.")

I'll get it!

(He moves to the front door upstage center.)

Who is it?

MARY

Room service!

(DRITHERS opens the door. MARY ENTERS with a covered tray and adds it to the buffet table.)

DRITHERS

It's Mary! What a surprise!

MARY

Evening, sir.

DRITHERS

Snooker. Looky here! It's Mary!

SNOOKER

I can see that.

DRITHERS

What a surprise!

SNOOKER

Oh, I'm all aghast.

MARY

Thank you, sir. I'll be going now.

DRITHERS

Going so soon?

SNOOKER

Douglas!?

DRITHERS

Right. Thank you, Mary. Most kind of you.

(MARY EXITS upstage center.)

SNOOKER

No more excuses now.

DRITHERS

Right!

(He moves downstage right to JULIE'S bedroom door. He pauses to gather his nerve. He raises his hand. As he draws his hand back to knock, there is a KNOCK on the front door upstage center. He again takes advantage of "the bell.")

I'll get it.

(He moves to the upstage center door.)

Who's there?

HANNIBAL

Room service!

(DRITHERS opens the door.)

Good evening, sir.

DRITHERS

What's so good about it?

HANNIBAL

I've come with the ice for the bar, sir.

DRITHERS

Yes, of course. It's about time. We are all out of ice. Come in.

(*HANNIBAL goes about his business.*)

SNOOKER

No more delays, Douglas.

DRITHERS

I didn't plan the interruptions.

SNOOKER

No, but you are using them quite well.

HANNIBAL

That was all, sir. I'll be back at seven o'clock for the party.

DRITHERS

Thank you.

HANNIBAL

My pleasure, sir.

(*He EXITS upstage center. DRITHERS and SNOOKER exchange a glance.*)

SNOOKER

We are running out of time!

DRITHERS

Right again.

(He moves again towards the bedroom door. He pauses, then raises his hand. As he draws his hand back to knock, there is a KNOCK on the upstage center door.)

SNOOKER

No, I'll get it!

(He moves to upstage center and opens the door to reveal BRIARBUSH.)

What do you want?

BRIARBUSH

(At the door.) Mr. Snooker! Mr. Drithers! How glad I am to see you together.

(He ENTERS.)

I know the party is scheduled to begin in a few minutes, but I have very pressing business.

DRITHERS

Mr. Briarbutt…

BRIARBUSH

…bush…

DRITHERS

Can't it wait?

BRIARBUSH

I'm afraid not. It concerns your daughter.

DRITHERS

Oh no! Not you, too.

BRIARBUSH

Mr. Drithers, sir! It has been brought to our attention that our competition in the Dallas hotel business has attempted to sabotage our hotel during your stay. They surely hope to ruin our business by destroying our reputation. But we have out-smarted the old jackals this time. We have caught the thief red-handed. He was dressed as a bellboy and had a box of chocolates with this card attached.

(He hands the card to DRITHERS.)

We presume he planned to deliver them to your daughter during the party.

DRITHERS

(He reads.) "To Julie. The woman of my dreams. From a secret admirer."

BRIARBUSH

I'm sure that it was the same person that Miss Julie found in her bed yesterday. It is more than obvious to me that his presence in your suite was nothing more than an act of sabotage. Now that we have the culprit in irons, I can assure you that the engagement party will not be interrupted. We have the situation completely in hand.

DRITHERS

Well, that explains a few things around here, at least.

BRIARBUSH

Further, Mr. McGruff is holding our saboteur just down the hall-way. I think it only appropriate that he make a personal apology to you before we call the police to come take him away. So, if you will allow…

DRITHERS

I really don't think…

(BRIARBUSH blows on his seaman's whistle three tones. Shortly afterwards McGRUFF ENTERS with BOBBY by the arm.)

McGRUFF

Come along now! No use fighting it.

BRIARBUSH

Mr. Drithers, I present to you the saboteur.

DRITHERS

Bobby Granger?!

BOBBY

Hello, Mr. Drithers, sir.

BRIARBUSH

What? You know this criminal?!

DRITHERS

Know him? The scoundrel works for me.

BRIARBUSH

You mean to say, you paid him to sabotage our hotel?!

DRITHERS

No, of course not. He's no more a saboteur than I am.

BRIARBUSH

Oh my!

McGRUFF

That means…

SNOOKER

…you've caught the wrong man.

DRITHERS

However, I am very grateful that you've brought this scoundrel to my doorstep. I had expected to find him in El Paso.

BOBBY

I can explain that, Mr. Drithers, sir…

DRITHERS

You had better, because there's a lot of explaining to be done here!

BRIARBUSH

Oh, this is awful! Just awful!

SNOOKER

You're telling me!?

BRIARBUSH

If this isn't our man, then the real saboteur...

SNOOKER

Assuming there ever was one.

McGRUFF

...is still on the loose...

BRIARBUSH

...doing his best to ruin my hotel! McGruff! Get downstairs right now! Don't let anyone in or out of the hotel.

McGRUFF

Right!

BRIARBUSH

Battle stations!

(McGRUFF EXITS upstage center.)

Oh, do pardon. I got carried away.

SNOOKER

Oh no, please. You handled that wonderfully. I'm impressed.

BRIARBUSH

Why, thank you.

SNOOKER

Don't mention it.

DRITHERS

Briarbutt!...

BRIARBUSH

...bush...

DRITHERS

...would you please keep your mouth shut. I have business to attend to and I'm running out of time.

BRIARBUSH

Right, sir!

DRITHERS

Now, where was I?

BOBBY

About my being in Dallas…

DRITHERS

Right! Well?

BOBBY

I was sent by the company's vice president in charge of production to deliver an envelope to you, sir. A message of importance concerning the new drilling sites. I have it here, if you would like to read it…

DRITHERS

Fine! You're here on business, are you? Would you like to explain why it has taken you so long to deliver it to me?…and since when do employees of Drithers Oil Incorporated wear "bellboy red" in the line of duty?…and what are you doing delivering candy to my daughter and sending her flowers?…and since when can you afford to send flowers to young ladies on the poverty wage that I pay you?

BOBBY

I suppose this means you're not interested in the letter right now?

DRITHERS

You scoundrel, you!

SNOOKER

Don't kill him, Douglas. You'll need him alive for the wedding.

DRITHERS

Young man! Do you know what a disgrace you have brought upon this family?! Upon my company? What may be left of it come December? Huh? You have disgraced me, as well as my daughter!

BOBBY

Sir! There must be some mistake...

DRITHERS

Oh yes. There's been a mistake all right. Although Julie isn't totally blameless in the affair, the mistake was yours!

BOBBY

Sir?

DRITHERS

Don't play innocent with me. I heard it all from Julie's own mouth. "Your right arm disrobing her...a thousand passionate kisses." Had I been there, you would have paid dearly!

BOBBY

Sir?! What are you trying to say?!

DRITHERS

As if you didn't know...

SNOOKER

Douglas, maybe he doesn't know.

DRITHERS

Maybe you're right.

BOBBY

Know what?

DRITHERS

Maybe she's kept it from him as well.

BOBBY

Kept what from me?

DRITHERS

Thanks to your thousand passionate kisses, the engagement of Julie and Matthew will not be possible.

BOBBY

Oh? Really? And why may I ask?

DRITHERS

Because Julie is pregnant with your child.

BRIARBUSH

My God!

BOBBY

Pregnant?…with my child? But that's not possible…

DRITHERS

What do you take me for? I'm not so easily duped. You are the father of this child and you'll make my daughter an honest woman through marriage—even if you have to do it looking up the barrel of my shotgun!

BOBBY

Marriage?

(BOBBY begins to catch on.)

DRITHERS

Or do you pretend to deny the allegations?

BOBBY

Oh no, not at all. I'm the father. I admit it. I'm the one. It was me. Oh, for shame, for shame. What have I done?!

DRITHERS

There! I don't see a need to confront Julie about this after all. Do you, Snooker?

SNOOKER

No. It's pretty much black and white to me. What do you want to do, Douglas?

DRITHERS

I'm not sure. Bobby, exactly how…pregnant is my daughter?

BOBBY

Oh, I'd say very pregnant.

DRITHERS

I mean to say, how many months along do you think she is?

BOBBY

Oh that. I'd say, seven…*(DRITHERS' jaw drops.)* eight…

DRITHERS

Eight?!

(Total disbelief and shock on DRITHERS' face. BOBBY realizes he's guessing too far in the wrong direction and thus changes course.)

BOBBY

…five…four?…*(The others look ready to believe it.)*…four months along. That's about right.

DRITHERS

Four months along!?

SNOOKER

She'll be showing any day now.

DRITHERS

That settles it. There's no time for an engagement. We'll have to go straight for the wedding. Today!

BOBBY

Today?!

DRITHERS

Any objections?

BOBBY

Oh, no. None at all. Today would be just fine. I mean, we don't want Miss Julie to carry this shame one day longer than necessary.

DRITHERS

I'd hope not.

BOBBY

Good. Then it's settled.

DRITHERS

Briarbutt!

BRIARBUSH

...bush...

DRITHERS

You go find us a minister or a Justice of the Peace or something.

BRIARBUSH

Sir? What about the engagement party?

DRITHERS

You heard me! We're not having an engagement party. We're having a wedding instead.

BRIARBUSH

Oh my!

DRITHERS

And hurry up about it.

BRIARBUSH

Right! There's a Baptist ministers' conference in the new wing. I'll see what I can arrange.

(He EXITS upstage center.)

DRITHERS

Snooker! Take Bobby back to your suite and see if you can find him something to wear for his wedding. Red isn't at all a good color for him.

SNOOKER

I'll see what I can rummage up. He and Matt are close to the same size. Maybe something from his wardrobe will fit.

DRITHERS

Fine. Keep him there until you hear Briairbutt's whistle. We'll have to keep this from Julie until the last possible moment.

SNOOKER

Come along young man. I'll have to warn you. Mrs. Snooker isn't at all happy about this new arrangement.

(After BOBBY and SNOOKER EXIT upstage center, JULIE ENTERS downstage right dressed for the party.)

JULIE

You're alone? I thought I heard voices.

DRITHERS

Just the hired help. They came to deliver the buffet.

JULIE

Oh, I thought I heard Mr. Snooker's voice.

DRITHERS

Oh, right. He just dropped by to say he would be a few minutes late. Nothing else, you understand.

JULIE

Daddy, why so nervous? It's my engagement party, not yours.

DRITHERS

Yes, well, I wanted to talk to you about that exact thing. You see, I've been thinking.

JULIE

What about, Daddy?

DRITHERS

About you and your future…your immediate future.

JULIE

And?

DRITHERS

I thought it would be wiser and more expedient, if we didn't wait so long after the engagement is announced to have the wedding.

JULIE

Oh?

DRITHERS

Yes. I know how things can get out of hand between the announcement of the engagement and the actual wedding.

JULIE

Oh really?

DRITHERS

Things can really look different a few months down the road. Amazing all that can come to light, if you give it a while. Little hidden problems can grow to really big problems that can't be hidden, if you understand what I mean?

JULIE

I'm not sure if I do.

DRITHERS

I'm sure that we will all benefit from an earlier wedding. I'm sure your mother would have wanted it that way.

JULIE

Daddy, I'm doing this for you, and for mother, because it makes you happy. If you think we should have a short engagement, then it's all right with me.

DRITHERS

Oh, I'm so glad to hear that.

JULIE

How long between the engagement and the wedding did you think appropriate?

DRITHERS

Oh, about five minutes.

JULIE

What?!

DRITHERS

You said you'd do it for me. You'll have to trust me on this, Julie. It really is for the best. We're arranging for the minister presently. You'll be married before the evening is over. There will be fewer questions asked this way.

JULIE

But Daddy?! I don't have a wedding dress!

DRITHERS

Your party dress will do splendidly.

JULIE

But I wanted to wear white.

DRITHERS

Now that's a bit far fetched!

JULIE

And what is that suppose to mean?

DRITHERS

Nothing! Nothing at all! Julie, dearest! Please trust me on this. It's best for everybody. We can talk about it in a couple of months when things come into focus. But for now, our guests are due any moment. Will you do this for me? I know it's asking a lot.

JULIE

Daddy!

DRITHERS

Please!

(Pause.)

JULIE

Oh, fine. What does it matter. Waiting three months doesn't make it any better. Fine, just fine. Whatever you want.

DRITHERS

Thank you, dearest. You won't regret this! It'll all make sense to you in the by-and-by.

JULIE

We'll wait and see.

DRITHERS

Julie, I know a wedding is supposed to be one of the more special moments in life and it may seem like you're being rushed into this whole thing...well, it seems that way because...well, because...you are!

(There is a KNOCK at the door.)

I'll get it.

(He moves upstage center and opens the door. MARY and HANNIBAL stand at the open door.)

MARY

Good evening sir!

HANNIBAL

Good evening, sir!

DRITHERS

Good evening. You're right on time. The first of the guests have yet to arrive.

(There is a KNOCK at the door.)

And so it begins. To your places, please.

MARY

Right away, sir!

(MARY moves to behind the buffet table. HANNIBAL moves to behind the bar. DRITHERS opens the door. BRIARBUSH stands at the door with JASPER, disguised as a Baptist minister, Rev. Smith.)

DRITHERS

Oh, it's you. Come in.

(BRIARBUSH and JASPER ENTER, closing the door behind them.)

BRIARBUSH

Good evening. I see our hotel personnel have arrived and are about their duties. Excellent! Excellent! Mr. Drithers, sir, may I introduce Reverend Smith. He's prepared to do the honors.

DRITHERS

Thank you, Reverend. I know it's short notice...

JASPER

It's my pleasure. I was a bit hesitant at first, but then Mr. Briarbush explained the whole thing to me. I'm always willing to help young people make things right, if you know what I mean?

DRITHERS

Yes, I do. Thank you again for helping out.

(There is a KNOCK at the door. DRITHERS opens the door. McGRUFF and FRANK, dressed as a reporter, stand at the door.)

McGRUFF

Good evening, sir.

(They ENTER.)

DRITHERS

Good evening. Who's that with you?

McGRUFF

A reporter for the local paper.

DRITHERS

I told you I didn't want any extra publicity. He should join the guests downstairs in the bar.

McGRUFF

Sir! If I may interject. He says he's heard some delicate rumors concerning Miss Julie. He has threatened to print the rumors as he heard them, if he is not allowed to cover the party.

DRITHERS

The nerve of that guy. Just who does he think he is?

McGRUFF

Sir, I don't think it would be wise to turn him away. The story is gonna come out anyway. It's best if you have some control over how it's reported.

DRITHERS

Fine! Just fine. Let him come in, but one wise crack from him and he is out on his ear!

McGRUFF

Good, sir. *(To the reporter.)* You can stay, but watch your step and keep your mouth shut.

FRANK

Hey, we're a friendly bunch of folks, aren't we?

(There is a KNOCK at the door.)

DRITHERS

Let me.

(He opens the door. SALLY and MATT ENTER upstage center.)

Hello Sally! and Matthew! I'm glad you chose to come. Please come on in.

SALLY

Thank you, Douglas. It's not what we had hoped for, but we feel it important to stand together as friends in these tough times.

DRITHERS

Thank you, Sally. I appreciate your condolences.

JULIE

What is going on here? I've been to funerals that were more festive than this.

DRITHERS

I'm sorry, dear. You're right. This is a wedding. It's a happy occasion. So let's get it over with, shall we?

JULIE

Daddy!

DRITHERS

Oh, sorry. I mean, let's get on with it. Julie, come stand next to me. Reverend Smith, if you please.

(He gestures him to take his place.)

Mr. Briarbutt?

BRIARBUSH

…bush…bush…Briarbush!

DRITHERS

Right, just like you want. The whistle please.

BRIARBUSH

…with pleasure, sir.

(He blows two long blasts and one short on his seaman's whistle. There is a moment of silence broken by the sound of footsteps. BRIARBUSH begins the first few bars of the wedding march on his whistle. As he plays, the

door opens. SNOOKER escorts BOBBY into the room. BOBBY is wearing MATT'S suit.)

JULIE

Bobby?!

(SNOOKER ushers him to JULIE'S side.)

DRITHERS

Reverend Smith, there's your man.

JASPER

Oh how wonderful. If the happy couple would join hands.

JULIE

Daddy?! What is going on here.

BOBBY

It's all right, Julie. They know all about it.

JULIE

About what?!

BOBBY

About us!

JULIE

What about us?

DRITHERS

Julie dearest. There's no need for me to pretend any longer, and you won't have to either. We know...well...everything. I wanted to force you to marry someone you didn't love. I'm responsible for the whole thing. Do you think I couldn't see through the smoke screen? I saw through it all. Considering your condition, I just couldn't see my way clear to make you marry someone else...someone you didn't love.

JULIE

Oh Daddy.

DRITHERS

I also know your nerves have not been exactly stable since this whole story began. All that talk about the bodies in your room...really now?!

JULIE

But Daddy...

BOBBY

It's all right, Julie. He knows all about it.

(He winks at JULIE.)

I've told him everything. There's nothing left to do but say "I do." You needn't pretend anymore.

JULIE

...pretend...oh!...pretend. Right! Oh Daddy...how thoughtful of you. You saw through my troubled disguise and made the arrangements for my wedding. Oh how sweet.

(JULIE still looks very confused, but thinks she understands and is follow-
ing BOBBY'S lead.)

DRITHERS

Now that's better. Your mother would be so proud of you, despite the circumstances.

JULIE

Circumstances?

DRITHERS

And that joke about wearing white at your wedding…*(He chuck-*
les.)…you thought I'd fall for that one…that was a good one. *(He chuckles again.)*

JULIE

(Aside to BOBBY.) What is he talking about?!

BOBBY

Ask me later. If you love me, just say "I do" when the time comes.

DRITHERS

Reverend Smith. Let's get on with it, shall we.

JASPER

Right-O. Dearly beloved. We are gathered here today to join together in holy matrimony Julie Drithers and Bobby Granger. Who gives this woman in marriage?

DRITHERS

(*Aside to SNOOKER.*) That's a good one. She's already been taken! (*He chuckles some more.*)

JULIE

(*Aside to BOBBY.*) What is wrong with him today?

BOBBY

If you love me, just play along. I'll explain it all later.

JASPER

Mr. Drithers? I believe that's your line. As the father of the bride, you get to say "I do."

DRITHERS

Oh right. Sorry. I guess I was sleeping. (*He clears his throat*) I do.

JASPER

If there is any reason that these two should not be wed, let him speak now or forever hold his peace.

(*A beat.*)

Excellent. I always find that part so exciting. You never know what some crackpot in the back row is gonna say.

DRITHERS

Keep it moving, Reverend. The champagne is getting warm.

JASPER

Right. Moving right along. Do you, Julie, take this man as your…huh…lawfully wedded husband, to have and to hold, to love and to cherish, in good times as in bad, in sickness and in health, and all that good stuff, 'til death do you part?

JULIE

I do!

JASPER

Do you, Bobby, take this woman as your lawfully wedded wife, to have and to hold, to love and to cherish, in good times as in bad, in sickness and in health, etcetera, etcetera, 'til death do you part?

BOBBY

I do.

JASPER

That's always my favorite part. It's so romantic! You may exchange the rings.

BOBBY

We don't have any rings.

JASPER

You don't have any rings?

JULIE

No! This was originally meant to be an engagement party.

JASPER

Oh, right again. I forgot. This was the last minute right-the-wrong ceremony. Well, we must have rings or the ceremony isn't complete.

HANNIBAL

Here! This might serve the purpose.

(HANNIBAL pulls the seals from two liquor bottles and passes them to DRITHERS.)

DRITHERS

(Examining the labels.) My favorite brand! Here you go. Let's get it over with now.

JASPER

You may now exchange the rings as a…uh…symbol of your ever-lasting love.

(They do so.)

You may now kiss the bride.

(They kiss.)

May I be the first to present to you, Mr. and Mrs. Bobby Granger.

(All applaud lightly.)

SNOOKER

Let's eat!

(He moves to the buffet table.)

DRITHERS

How about something to drink first?!

(He moves to the bar.)

SALLY

My best wishes to you both. Please ignore the men folk. They've had a bit too much to drink.

JULIE

Thank you, Mrs. Snooker. I'm afraid I still don't understand this whole thing. I expected an engagement party and got a whirlwind wedding instead…to an altogether unexpected groom.

SALLY

A whirlwind wedding, you say?…I call it more of a shotgun wedding. All the same, we wish you the very best.

(JULIE looks more puzzled than ever. BOBBY cuts in before she can speak.)

BOBBY

Thank you, Mrs. Snooker. Very kind indeed.

(SALLY moves to the buffet table.)

JULIE

(Aside to BOBBY.) What did she mean by "shotgun wedding"? Did my father force you to marry me?

BOBBY

No, not at all. I just took advantage of his insistence, that's all. Do you really think anyone would have to use force? I've wanted nothing more than to marry you! You know that!

JULIE

But…What is going on here?!

(BRIARBUSH and McGRUFF move to congratulate the couple.)

BRIARBUSH

Congratulations to you both! What an exciting week it has been. First to have you and your father here as honored guests in our hotel and then to be here at your wedding! How marvelous! Simply marvelous.

McGRUFF

I couldn't agree with Mr. Briarbush more! Congratulations Mrs. Granger, Mr. Granger. It has been a privilege.

(SNOOKER moves from the buffet table to congratulate the couple.)

SNOOKER

Congratulations, dearest Julie! And to you, Mr. Granger. I wish you the very best for your future. I want a cigar when that first little one shows up! Do ya hear?!

BOBBY

Yes sir! You can count on it.

DRITHERS

Congratulations, Bobby. Take good care of her. Congratulations, Julie. I hope you're happy with my choice of grooms. And I hope you're not too unhappy with me for all this…

JULIE

Nonsense, Daddy! You've made me very happy. Thank you, but I still don't understand why the rush and the last minute changes. Would you please explain yourself now. If you had just told me, it would have all been so much easier.

DRITHERS

Sure, sure. As if you didn't know. *(He chuckles.)* You know, at first it really bothered me, but the more I think about becoming a grandfather, the more I like it, And why not?! I can see myself bouncing that precious little tot on my knee...playing horsy...and feeding him his bottle...

JULIE

Oh Daddy, aren't you rushing things a little? I'm sure we'll have kids in time; why we've not even had a chance to discuss family plans together. I'm sure that the first one won't be here for years still!

DRITHERS

Julie, you needn't pretend anymore.

JULIE

Pretend?! Pretend what?

DRITHERS

Oh come now, we all know that you've a little bun in the oven.

JULIE

A what?!

DRITHERS

A rug rat on the way! A baby in the basket! Julie dearest, we know that you're expecting—that you're pregnant!

JULIE

Pregnant?! But I'm not pregnant!

DRITHERS

You're not?

SNOOKER

You're not?

MATT

You're not?

JULIE

No! Of course not!

JASPER

She's not?!

MARY

She's not?!

SALLY

She's not!!

JULIE

(To DRITHERS.) Who told you that?!

DRITHERS

Well,…well, Snooker did!

JULIE

What does he know about it?

SNOOKER

Well, I heard it from Sally!

JULIE

And? Since when is Sally an expert on my reproductive processes?

SALLY

Oh my! Matthew told me that you were…

MATT

Mr. McGruff brought it to my attention.

McGRUFF

I…I…

JULIE

Well?!

McGRUFF

I heard it from Mr. Briarbush.

DRITHERS

Did you now?!

JULIE

And where did you hear about it?

BRIARBUSH

I can explain…

JULIE

Where did you hear about it?!

BRIARBUSH

From Hannibal, the Bellboy.

JULIE

The Bellboy?! Well of all the nerve…

HANNIBAL

I heard it from the maid!

JULIE

And who did you hear it from, my dearest!

MARY

I heard it from the reporter there, but he wasn't a reporter when he told it to me. He was a bellboy.

BRIARBUSH

A bellboy!

McGRUFF

A bellboy!!

FRANK

So, gentlemen, it's been a wonderful wedding, but I do have a publication deadline and must be going now!

(He runs for the door.)

McGRUFF

Why the hurry, Mr. Reporter, sir?

FRANK

Like I said, I have an article to write.

BRIARBUSH

Which newspaper did you say you represent?

FRANK

The Times-Herald?

McGRUFF

And since when do reporters from the Times-Herald wear bellboy uniforms.

FRANK

There must be some mistake...

BRIARBUSH

I'm sure there is! What did you say your name was?

FRANK

I didn't.

BRIARBUSH

As I thought. Mr. Drithers, sir. We'll escort this bellboy/reporter downstairs. I'm sure the police will be very pleased to take him off our hands. We'll keep you informed of the proceedings.

(They start to exit upstage center.)

DRITHERS

Thank you.

FRANK

Hey, no police, please. I don't want any trouble...

McGRUFF

Come along now.

FRANK

Jasper! Help me! Jasper, say something.

(They stop and look towards the Reverend.)

JASPER

May the good Lord give you light on your way...or something like that.

FRANK

Jasper!

DRITHERS

Hold it, McGruff!

McGRUFF

Sir?

DRITHERS

Do you know this fellow, Reverend?

JASPER

No, of course not. I just wanted to...have mercy on a sinner.

FRANK

Jasper!

DRITHERS

(To FRANK.) Do you know this person from some other place besides the church?

FRANK

Church?! That no good skunk hasn't set foot in a church since he was twelve.

JASPER

If thy tongue sin against thee, then cut it out! Unless thou be cast into prison...uh...hell.

DRITHERS

I think that was a hand and an eye.

JASPER

I could be mistaken.

FRANK

Jasper, I ain't gonna cut my tongue out for nobody. If they're gonna take me, I'll make sure they know everything.

DRITHERS

McGruff! Take our Reverend away, too! They're obviously working together.

JASPER

How dare you insult a man of the cloth?

McGRUFF

Save it for the judge. I don't want to hear it.

FRANK

A fine mess you've got us into this time, Jasper.

JASPER

Keep your mouth shut, you moron.

BRIARBUSH

(To FRANK.) Who do you work for? Who hired you to try and damage the reputation of this fine hotel? Huh? Who's behind this whole plot? The Sheraton? The Hilton chain?

FRANK

The owner of the Dallas Regency Hotel.

BRIARBUSH

The Regency!? That no good Andrew Warner. I should have known.

FRANK

Yes, that's the guy! Jasper and I were promised a big bonus...

JASPER

Frank, hold your tongue!

FRANK

…that's right, a big bonus if we could stop Mr. Drithers here from buying into the Grand Hotel.

DRITHERS

Buying into the Grand? Me?! That's a laugh! I haven't any intentions of buying into any hotel at all.

FRANK

You don't?

JASPER

You don't?

BRIARBUSH

You don't?

DRITHERS

No, of course not.

FRANK

Hey, Jasper. We might get our bonus yet!

JASPER

Don't count on it, you stool pigeon.

BRIARBUSH

You mean you aren't interested in at least investing in the Grand Hotel?

DRITHERS

Hah! With what? I'm as broke as can be!

JULIE

What?!

SNOOKER

Now you've done it!

DRITHERS

Hey, no real damage done! Julie isn't pregnant after all, what a relief. It was just a great big practical joke.

JULIE

Daddy?!

DRITHERS

(*Ignoring her.*) But that's even better! If you're here to stop me from buying a hotel that I don't want to buy, that means you're not really a Reverend at all.

JULIE

Daddy?!

DRITHERS

And if you're not a real Reverend, then you can't legally perform a marriage ceremony. And if you can't perform a legal marriage ceremony, then Julie and Bobby aren't really married! Which means, Matt and Julie can still be married!!

(To BOBBY.)

Get away from my daughter!

(He pulls BOBBY from his place at his daughter's side. JULIE grabs BOBBY and pulls him back to her side.)

JULIE

You stay right where you are! Daddy!! I have a bone to pick with you!

DRITHERS

Daughter!

JULIE

Don't you daughter me! I've had my fill of that today! Are you broke or not?! The truth!

DRITHERS

Julie, I meant to talk to you about it all, right after the merger, I mean, wedding.

JULIE

So, Bobby was right. How dare you arrange my engagement with Matthew only to benefit your company's business?!

DRITHERS

Julie, please! Not here.

JULIE

Yes here! Was this whole arrangement made in order to merge your company together with Mr. Snooker's?!

DRITHERS

Please daughter, let me explain!

JULIE

Was I really nothing more than one more company asset to you in this whole ridiculous ordeal?!

DRITHERS

Julie!

JULIE

Yes or no?!!

DRITHERS

Yes…and I'm sorry.

JULIE

And did you change the engagement party into a wedding only because you thought I was expecting?

DRITHERS

Yes…and I'm sorry.

JULIE

Without even the courtesy of talking to me about it first?! If you had just knocked at my door and asked me!

SNOOKER

I warned you, old man!

JULIE

Mother would have been ashamed of you. How could you?!

FRANK

This is getting really good, huh, Jasper!

DRITHERS

(To McGRUFF.) Would you get those two out of here!

McGRUFF

Right sir! Right away! Out you go! You've overstayed your welcome this time.

(McGRUFF, JASPER and FRANK EXIT upstage center.)

DRITHERS

Julie, I am sorry. I don't know what to say. I'm ashamed.

JULIE

Well, I know what to say. I hereby announce my intent to become Mrs. Bobby Granger. Mr. Briarbush! Would you please go downstairs to the bar and restaurant and ask the invited party guests to come on up to the cattleman's suite. The engagement party is about to begin!

BRIARBUSH

With pleasure, Miss Julie!

(He EXITS upstage center.)

JULIE

Any objections, Daddy?!

DRITHERS

No. None at all. Let me be the first to congratulate you on your choice of husbands.

JULIE

Oh Daddy!

(They hug.)

SNOOKER

Well, Douglas, old boy. We tried.

DRITHERS

We tried. I wonder how it will feel to be flat broke?

BOBBY

Mr. Drithers, sir! I think I can be of some help. I've been trying to deliver this letter since yesterday morning.

DRITHERS

Young man, this isn't the time for business. Can't you see that I need a drink?

BOBBY

It's important, sir. Please, give it a look.

DRITHERS

Very well.

(He takes the envelope and begins to read, silently at first, then aloud.)

"We knew you'd want to know without delay…we struck oil on the Johnson property…the biggest strike since thirty-six…" Why didn't you give this to me sooner?!

BOBBY

I tried, sir, but you were busy…

DRITHERS

I'm rich! I'm rich! I can't believe it! Snooker! Can you believe it. I see a merger on the horizon! My company and yours!

SNOOKER

My debts and yours! I can hear the stocks rising already!

DRITHERS

Snooker, we did it! We did it!

(They hug.)

TOGETHER

"Frog legs, frog legs, hop to the top! All the way to graduate, we're never gonna stop!"

DRITHERS

What are we gonna call the soon-to-be merged company of our, anyway?

SNOOKER

Since it's your money, how about "Drithers Oil and Pipe Incorporated"?

(They laugh.)

DRITHERS

That sounds mighty fine! Mr. Granger! Son-in-law-to-be! As soon as the merger is complete and the confidence in our stock is reestablished, I'm taking my retirement. From then on, you're the boss at Drithers Oil and Pipe Incorporated.

BOBBY

Oh, thank you, Mr. Drithers, sir!

DRITHERS

Call me Dad!

BOBBY

Yes sir! Dad, sir!

JULIE

Oh Daddy!

DRITHERS

You know, Julie. Now that the company is solvent again, I think I just might be interested in buying a hotel after all.

JULIE

Oh really?

DRITHERS

Yes. I think I just might buy the Dallas Grand Hotel after all. It might be a very enjoyable venture. Snook', old pal? Do you think Matt would be interested in managing a fine hotel like this one?

SNOOKER

I'm sure he would be thrilled.

(BRIARBUSH ENTERS alone upstage center.)

BRIARBUSH

The guests are on their way up!

SNOOKER

What about him?

DRITHERS

Right! *(A beat.)* Mr. Briarbush.

BRIARBUSH

...butt...butt...Briarbutt!

DRITHERS

As you wish.

BRIARBUSH

Sir?

DRITHERS

You're fired.

(All laugh. The sounds of the guests arriving can be heard in the hallway as...)

THE CURTAIN FALLS

0-595-24285-5